Orangeville Ontario Part 2 and Area in Photos, Saving Our History One Photo at a Time

Photography
by Barbara Raué
2013

Series Name:
Cruising Ontario

Book 31: Orangeville Part 2 and Area

Cover photo: Eagle Carving in front of 299 Broadway Avenue

Series Name: Cruising Ontario

Book 1: London
Book 2: Dundas
Book 3: Hamilton
Book 4: Oakville
Book 5: Chesley
Book 6: Stoney Creek
Book 7: Waterdown
Book 8: Owen Sound
Book 9: Mount Forest
Book 10: Dundalk
Book 11: Burford and Area
Book 12: Waterford and Area
Book 13: Drumbo and Area
Book 14: Sheffield and Area
Book 15: Tavistock and Area
Book 16: Ancaster and Mount Hope
Book 17: Innerkip
Book 18: Brantford
Book 19: Burlington
Book 20: Guelph and Area
Book 21: Ayr
Book 22: Erin
Book 23: Goderich
Book 24: Lucknow and Area
Book 25: Paris
Book 26: Toronto
Book 27: Beaver Valley
Book 28: Collingwood
Book 29: Peterborough
Book 30: Orangeville Beginnings Part 1
Book 31: Orangeville Part 2 and Area
Book 32: Port Elgin

Other Books by Barbara Raue

Coins of Gold

Arrows, Indians and Love

The Life and Times of Barbara
Volume 1: Inventions That Have Enhanced My Life
Volume 2: Entertainment That I Have Enjoyed
Volume 3: East Coast Trips
Volume 4: Olympics Have Always Intrigued Me
Volume 5: Wonders of the World
Volume 6: Caribbean Cruises We Have Enjoyed
Volume 7: Animals
Volume 8: Storms and Other Major Disasters in My Lifetime
Volume 9: Wars, Terrorist Attacks and Major Disasters

The Cromwell Family Book

Orangeville

In 1837 James Griggs bought 100 acres on the south side of what is now Broadway and built the first mill on Mill Creek. In 1843, Orange Lawrence bought 300 acres along with Griggs' mill; he opened a general store, built a second mill, started the first school, and in 1847 he was the first postmaster. In 1857 two sons-in-law of Orange Lawrence, Thomas Jull and John Walker Reid built a mill at the corner of Mill and Armstrong Streets. In 1863 Orangeville was incorporated as a village in Wellington County with a population of 1200. By 1871 two daily stage lines were operating between Orangeville and Brampton and in the same year the Toronto, Grey and Bruce Railway, a narrow gauge rail line, reached Orangeville. In 1885 telephones were installed in Orangeville, but it wasn't until 1916 that electricity came to the town.

Caledon Village

Caledon is located northwest of Brampton. Caledon Village is one of the small communities in the town of Caledon.

Laurel

The hamlet of Laurel is located on the 5th Line (or Country Road 12) in the Township of Amaranth.

Mono Centre

Mono is a rural community of rolling, tree-covered hills with streams and creeks forming the headwaters of the Humber, Nottawasaga and Credit Rivers. Mono Centre Post Office was open from 1851 to 1969. The Turnbull and Henry families settled here in 1823. The village included a general store, library, hotel, blacksmith, grist mill, saw mill, wagon maker, church, and township hall.

Table of Contents

Zina Street

Primitive Methodist Church – 3 Zina Street – built in 1867, a simple Gothic structure with buff brick buttresses separating the segmented lancet windows

Rose window

2-6 Zina Street – Queen Anne style with decorative brick panels under the windows and buff brick soldiering topping the windows. Each unit of the row houses has a two-and-a-half storey tower-like bay with projecting eaves and large fretwork pieces resembling brackets. The transom over the off centre doors helps to lighten the interior hallways.

7 Zina Street – built in 1890 using all buff-coloured brick, the home of Jeremiah Dodds, a pharmacist. The style is an interpretation of Victorian Gothic with highly decorated vergeboards and Queen Anne influences in the rectangular windows and heavy stone lintels.

14 Zina – a similar buff brick home built a few years later than 7 Zina, built for merchant John Thompson

11 Zina – Gothic Revival style with an L-shaped floor plan, front gable and simple lancet window – the wide arch-topped windows topped with transoms came into fashion later in the century. The porch has 1920s features indicating the home has been modified over the years.

17 Zina Street

19 Zina – Gothic Revival

25 Zina – home of Eliza and James Robinson, Carpenter – 1885

28 Zina - Italianate home built in 1881 by James McDonald with the belvedere topping the hipped roof to bring light into the attic – a rare feature in Orangeville

27 Zina – Edwardian Classicism built in 1923 with large triangular front gable with Palladian window and shallow roofed porch

26 Zina

A uniquely shaped roof line – 30 Zina

29-31 Zina Street

32-36 Zina Street

#31 – Gothic Revival

33 Zina – Gothic Revival – dichromatic brickwork, lighter coloured voussoirs

41 Zina – Gothic Revival – larger windows added on first floor
Built in 1877

56 Zina – Robert Hewitt, mason and contractor, c. 1876
Italianate style

45 Zina Street – Gothic Revival- picture taken in 2011

The same house taken in 2013 with new landscaping – what a transformation. Buff brick banding, decorative bargeboard, simple lancet window in the additional front gable. The porch has been altered probably after 1920 – the short brick piers with squared columns reflect Edwardian Classicism common at that time.

Dufferin County Court House, 51 Zina Street
Classic Revival style built in 1880 with three towers that project from the
façade, the centre one most prominent; buff brick for decorative window
hoods, bands, panels; cornice and capitals on red brick pilasters; projecting
gable ends with triangular pediments and decorated tympanums

62 Zina – Italianate – paired cornice brackets, buff coloured voussoirs and
banding

64 Zina Street – Italianate – paired cornice brackets, buff coloured voussoirs and dentil moulding

63 Zina Street – Italianate style - 1880
Agnes and Reverend John M. McIntyre, Presbyterian Minister

65 Zina – Italianate style – paired cornice brackets, buff-coloured voussoirs

67 Zina – Gothic Revival style with sharply-pitched gables, detailed vergeboards, dichromatic brickwork

Italianate

76 Zina – cottage

Italianate style

6 Zina Street - Gothic cottage

81 Zina Street – Italianate style

Victorian Gothic with decorated vergeboards and Queen Anne
influences in rectangular windows and heavy stone lintels

Clara Street

8 Clara Street – Gothic Revival – fancy bargeboard,
dichromatic brickwork – Joseph Riddell, Veterinarian - 1883

67 Clara Street – Gothic Revival

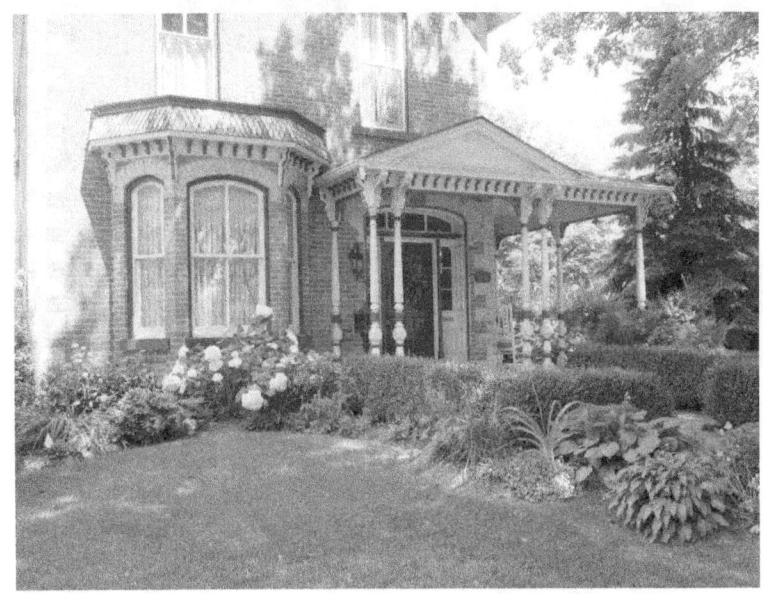

Bay window, narrow decorative porch pillars

73 Clara Street – Italianate – paired cornice brackets

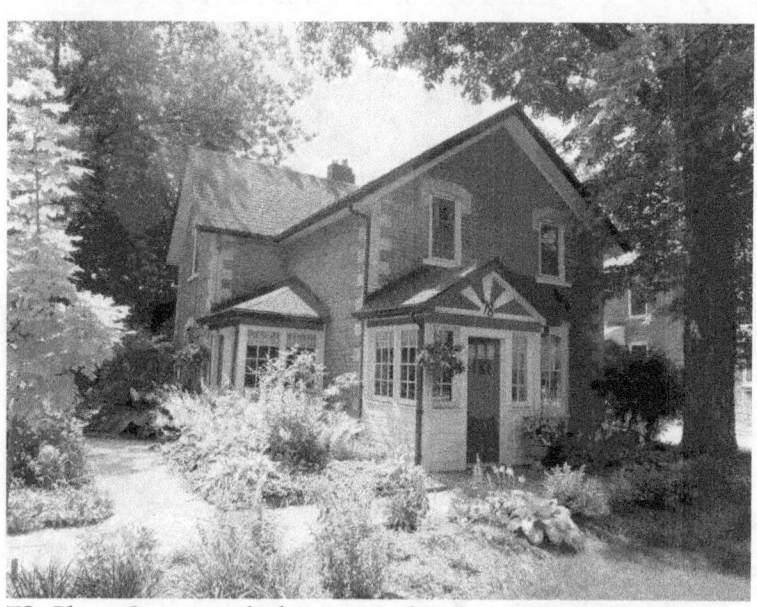

78 Clara Street – dichromatic brickwork, buff coloured voussoirs

98 Clara Street – Gothic Revival

Elizabeth Street

49 Elizabeth Street – Gothic Revival

24 Elizabeth Street – Oddfellows Hall Association

14 Second Street

Alexandra Park was named after Queen Alexandra consort of King Edward VII who succeeded his mother Queen Victoria in January 1901. The park, opened in August 1903, was built on the site of the former town stockyards which held cattle brought to the weekly market at the Town Hall. In 1923 the Dufferin County War Memorial was constructed in the park. The park originally wrapped around the Town Hall and out to Broadway. In 1932 the Town sold off the Broadway footage for a creamery and cold storage facility.

1 First Avenue – Gothic Revival – The John Green House built in 1875. Green owned a general store at Broadway and First Street, owned 111 acres with two houses, three shops, and two barns.

5 First Avenue – St. Mark's Anglican Church established in 1837 – the present church building was erected in 1868.

Gothic Revival – decorative dichromatic brickwork, paired cornice brackets, cornice return on the gables

10 First Avenue with old livery behind it

Apartment building beside livery taken from the alley

9 First Avenue – Gothic Revival – decorative bargeboard on the gable, decorative voussoir and keystone brickwork above the door

12-14 First Avenue – Gothic Revival – paired cornice brackets, verandahs

14 First Avenue – bargeboard on gable

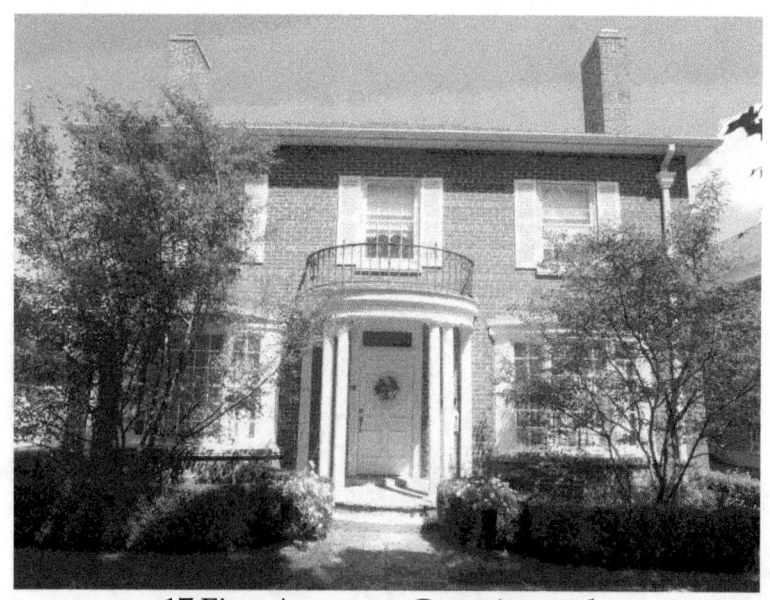

17 First Avenue – Georgian style

19 First Avenue

25 First Avenue – Gothic Revival
Robert Irvine, painter – c. 1885
Irvine House Bed and Breakfast

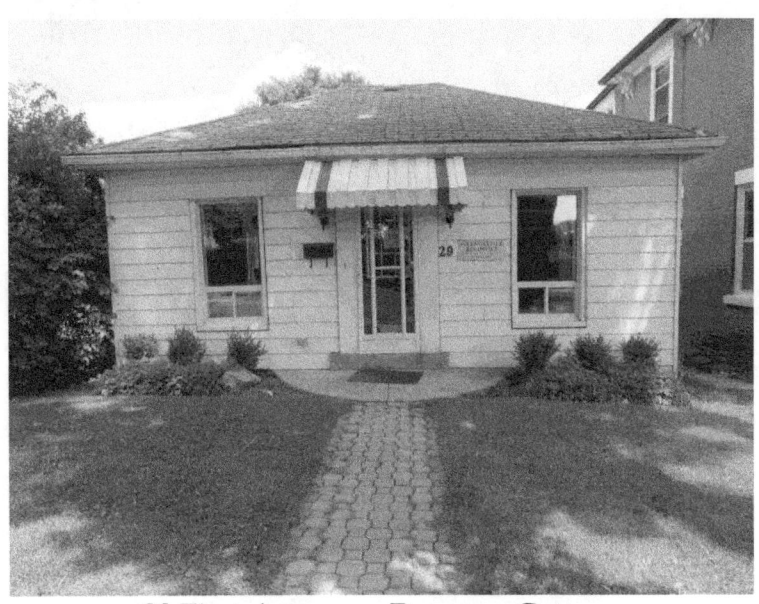

29 First Avenue – Regency Cottage
Orangeville BIA Office

31 First Avenue

34 First Avenue – Gothic Revival

First Street

5 First Street – Art Moderne style with flat roof, glass block windows, curved corners – built by Fred Webb c. 1944 and housed the Orangeville Dairy and Dairy Bar until 1969

15-17 First Street

18 First Street

20 First Street

22 First Street – Italianate style with wide bracketed eaves, wrap-around verandah, triangular pediment with decorated tympanum

31 First Street – Italianate – paired cornice brackets

33 First Street – modified Georgian style

39 First Street – Italianate

51 First Street – Italianate style

50 First Street – Gothic Revival – steeply pitched gable,
dichromatic brickwork

44 First Street – Gothic Revival with lighter-coloured decorative brickwork

46 First Street

1st Line and Highway 9 – Romanesque style – decorative vergeboard on gable, paired cornice brackets, quoining on centre tower and corners, rounded window vouissors with keystones

Cornice return on gable ends

Sculptures in Orangeville

Statue of Orange Lawrence
Founder, on island on Broadway

Remembrance Carving in
Alexandra Park

The first tree was carved in 2003. The sculptures are about art and community. Carvers create animals, historical figures, men, women, and tree spirits.

Great Horned Owl
Clara at Zina Street
Artist Tim Braithwaite

The Judge
62 Zina Street

The Prince of Wales
First and Zina Streets

Artist Jim Menken

The Musicians sculpture in Alexandra Park (just north of the Town Hall) is a tribute to the 10th anniversary of the Orangeville Blues and Jazz Festival in 2012. On musician is playing a harmonica (Blues) and the second musician is playing a saxophone (Jazz). Created by local artist Jim Menken.

The Eagle
Clara St. near Zina
Artist Jim Menken

The Lady
4 Clara Street
Artist Paul Frenette

The Boxer
64 Broadway

The Storyteller at library

Marilyn Harding Doekes was an elementary school teacher and Resource Librarian for over 30 years. She enjoyed sharing stories with the children and was in demand as a "storyteller" at school, at church, in people's homes and at community events. Artist Jim Menken in 2006

Amaranth   Letter Carrier Alexander Dunlop McKitrick
Lions Club   216 Broadway   255 Broadway
        Artist Jim Menken   Artist Peter Mogensen

Victorian Lady   The Indian   Tribute to Dogs
7 Zina Street   255 Broadway   65 Zina Street
Artist Robbin Wenzoski   Jeff Waters   Jim Menken

Canadian Nature   The Fiddler   Dr.A.G.Campbell
-a bear, woodpecker,   257 Broadway   21 York Street
two owls   Artist Nick Onac   rtist Peter Mogensen

Eagle on Nest
60 Mill Street
Artist Peter Turrell

Owl in Tree
61 Broadway
Artist Rob McFaul

The Dancer
40 Broadway
Bobbi Switzer

The Wizard
and Dragon
38 Broadway
Artist Paul Frenette

Canoe & Jack Pine
25 Broadway
Artist Nick Hall

Lumberjack
Broadway
across from
McDonald's

New carving at the Information Centre

Physician and
Patient
100 Rolling Hills
Drive (Hospital)
Artist Jim Menken

The Nurse
IODE's 100th
anniversary in
2007 – sits in
front of former
Hospital 32 First St
Artist Jim Menken

Helping Hands &
Caring Hearts
Elizabeth Street
Mrs. Baniulis
spent many years
as nurse and caring
for seniors

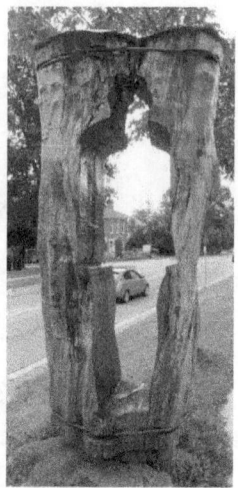

Moose with   The Dentist   The Hunter
Attitude   19 McCarthy St.   48 First Street
McCarthy St.   outside home of   Artist Don Miller
Artist Bob DeVries   Dentist John Russell
     Artist Jim Menken

Canadian Fighting Spirits   The Smile
(dedicated to Canadian troops   33 First Street
in Afghanistan) 48 First St.   Artist Robbin Wenzoski
Artist Murray Berger

Tree Spirit
267 Broadway
Artist Colin Partridge

Waving Bear
11 First Street

The Angel
9 McCarthy St.

Artist Walter vanderWindt

Carving at
Alexandra Park

Eagle at 299 Broadway

Caledon Village

Knox United Church – A.D. 1873

Regency Cottage in red brick with quoining on the corners,
buff coloured voussoirs

Buff coloured banding and on corners and voussoirs

Old Caledon Township Hall – A.D. 1875 – used as a court house, hall, library, now a theatre for Caledown Town Hall Players. The rectangular, gable-roofed building, with its red brick construction, decorative buff brick detailing and rounded multi-pane windows, shows municipal architecture of the 1870s.

Caledon Mountain Veterinary Hospital – 29 Elizabeth Street –
Italianate with single cornice brackets (double at corners),
heavy stone window lintels

Laurel

Laurel Gospel Hall – Gothic style, dichromatic brickwork,
lancet windows

Gothic Revival – decorative vergeboard on gable, dichromatic
brickwork, decorative rectangular window lintels

Edwardian Classicism – simple roof line, front porch, smooth red brick surfaces, paired cornice brackets, stone lintels above windows

Mono Centre

Burns United Church founded in 1837 by Scottish settlers

The Mono Cliffs Inn

Regency Cottage – buff coloured quoining at the corners

Belvedere: (from the Italian "beautiful view") an architectural feature on a roof, in a garden or on a terrace that gives a beautiful view. Example: 28 Zina Street	
Brackets: a decorative or weight-bearing structural element which forms a right angle with one side against a wall and the other under a projecting surface such as an eave or roof. Example: 34 Mill Street	
Buttress: a masonry structure built against or projecting from a wall which serves to support or reinforce the wall. In Canadian architecture, they are sometimes used for decoration. Example: 3 Zina Street	
Cornice: originally the wooden overhand of the roof. With the use of stone, brick, iron and steel, the cornice is any projecting shelf at the top of a ceiling or roof. They can be very decorative. Example: 117-123 Broadway	
Cupola: a small, dome-like structure on top of a building often used to provide a lookout or to admit light and air. Example: 87 Broadway (Town Hall)	
Dentil Moulding: an even series of rectangles used as ornamental decoration in cornices. Example: 187-192 Broadway	

Dichromatic brickwork: the use of two colours of brick, tile or slate to decorate a façade.	
Dormer: (French for "sleep") a gable end window that pierces through the plane of a sloping roof surface to create usable space in the top floor or attic of a building by adding headroom. Example: 135-139 Broadway	
Gable: the triangular portion of a wall between the edges of a sloping roof. Example: 16 York Street	
Gambrel Roof: a symmetrical two-sided roof with two slopes on each side; the upper slope is positioned at a shallow angle, while the lower slope is steep. It is similar to a mansard roof, but a gambrel has vertical gable ends instead of being hipped at the four corners of the building. Example: 239 Broadway	
Hipped Roof: a roof where all sides slope downwards to the walls with no gables. Example: 34 Mill Street	
Keystones and Voussoirs: a voussoir is a wedge-shaped element used in building an arch. A keystone is the central stone that locks all the stones into position, allowing the arch to bear weight. A keystone is often enlarged and embellished. Example: 117-123 Broadway	

Lancet Window: a tall, narrow window with a pointed arch at its top. Example: 3 Zina Street	
Mansard Roof: This style was popularized by Francois Mansart (1598-1666), an accomplished architect of the French Baroque period and especially fashionable during the Second French Empire (1852-1870). This roof is almost flat on the top section, with two slopes on each of its sides with the lower slope at a steeper angle than the upper and having dormer windows. Example: 16/18 Wellington Street	
Palladian Window: a large window that is divided into three sections with the centre section larger than the two side sections and usually arched. Example: 24 Zina Street	
Pediment: a triangular section above the horizontal structure (entablature), typically supported by columns. The inside of the triangle is called the tympanum. Example: 51 Zina Street	
Pilaster: a slightly projecting column built into or applied to the face of a wall for additional structural support. Example: 148 Broadway	
Quoin: masonry blocks at the corner of a wall, often a decorative feature, usually larger or of a different colour than the rest of the wall. Example: 6 York Street	

Rose Window: a circular window with ornamental tracery radiating from the centre. Example: 3 Zina Street	
Sidelight: a window, usually with a vertical emphasis, that flanks a door, and is often used to emphasize the importance of a primary entrance. Example: 14 Second Street, or 238 Broadway	
Vergeboards: also called bargeboards – hang from the projecting end of a roof and are often elaborately carved and ornamented. Example: 16 York Street	

Orangeville's Building Styles

Georgian, before 1860 – This style began with the British King Georges in the 18th century. These buildings have balanced facades around a central door, medium-pitched gable roofs, and small paned windows. Example: 260 Broadway	
Regency Cottage, 1830-1860 – This style originated in England in 1815 and spread to Ontario later in the 19th century as British officers retired to Canada. It is a modest one-storey house with a low-pitched hip roof and has a symmetrical front façade. Example: 11 First Street	
Gothic Revival, 1830-1890 – These decorative buildings have sharply-pitched gables with highly detailed vergeboards, pointed-arch window openings, and dichromatic brickwork. It is a common style in Ontario. Examples: 20 Wellington Street, 67 Zina Street	
Italianate, 1850-1900 – It has wide-bracketed eaves, belvederes, wrap-around verandahs. Examples: 12 York Street, 62 Zina Street	
Second Empire, 1860-1880 – The mansard roof is the most noteworthy feature of this style and is evidence of the French origins. Projecting central towers and one or two-storey bays can also be present. Example: 16-18 Wellington Street	
Romanesque Revival, 1880-1910 – This style hearkens back to medieval architecture of the 11th and 12th centuries with a heavy appearance, blocky towers and rounded arches. Example: 2 York Street	

Queen Anne, 1885-1900 – This style is distinguished by an irregular outline featuring a combination of an offset tower, broad gables, projecting two-storey bays, verandahs, multi-sloped roofs, and tall, decorative chimneys. A mixture of brick and wood is common. Windows often have one large single-paned bottom sash and small panes in the upper sash. Example: 239 Broadway	
Edwardian, 1900-1930 – This style bridges the ornate and elaborate styles of the Victorian era and the simplified styles of the 20th century. Balanced facades, simple roof lines, dormer windows, large front porches, and smooth brick surfaces are its characteristics. Example: 24 Zina Street	
Art Moderne, 1930-1945 – This style originated in the United States with rounded corners, smooth walls, and flat roofs. Large expanses of glass were used, even wrapping around corners. Example: former Orangeville Dairy, 5 First Street	